Introductory Essay on the Manichaean Heresy

Introductory Essay on the Manichaean Heresy

St. Augustine

Introductory Essay on the Manichaean Heresy

© Lighthouse Publishing 2017

Written by: St. Augustine (Nov.13 354 – Aug.28 430)

Translated by: Albert H. Newman. D.D., LL.D. (1852 – 1933)

Updated into Modern U.S English by A.M. Overett (b. 1960)

All rights reserved. Without limiting the rights under copyright reserved above, no part of this publication may be reproduced, stored in a retrieval system, or transmitted, in any form or by any means (electronic, mechanical, photocopying, recording or otherwise), without the prior written permission of the copyright owner of this book.

Published by
Lighthouse Christian Publishing
SAN 257-4330
5531 Dufferin Drive
Savage, Minnesota, 55378
United States of America

www.lighthousechristianpublishing.com

Introductory Notice.

This fourth volume of St. Augustin's Works contains his polemical writings in vindication of the Catholic Church against the heresy of the Manichæans, and the schism of the Donatists. The former are contained in Tom. II. and VIII., the latter in Tom. IX., of the Benedictine edition. Like the preceding volumes, this also is more than a reprint of older translations, and contains important additions not previously published. I.—Seven Writings Against the Manichæan Heresy. Four of these were translated by the Rev. Richard Stothert, of Bombay, for Dr. Dods' edition, published by T. & T. Clark, Edinburgh, 1872, and revised by Dr. Albert H. Newman, of Toronto, for the American edition. The other three treatises are translated, I believe for the first time, by Dr. Newman for this edition. (See Contents.) The Edinburgh translation, especially of the first two treatises, is sufficiently faithful and idiomatic, and needed very little alteration by the American editor, who compared it sentence by sentence with the Latin original, and made changes only where they seemed necessary. This part of the volume is also enriched by an introductory essay of Dr. Newman, which embodies the literature and the results of the most recent as well as the earlier researches concerning that anti-Christian heresy. II.—The Writings Against the Donatists. These were well translated by the Rev. J. R. King, of Oxford, and are slightly revised by Dr. Hartranft, of Hartford, after a careful comparison with the Latin. The literary introduction of Dr. Hartranft, regarding the translator's historical preface, will place the reader in the situation of the controversy between the Catholic Church and the Donatists at the time of St. Augustin. In both sections the treatises are arranged in chronological order. The fifth volume will contain the writings of St. Augustin against the Pelagians and Semi-Pelagians.

Chapter I.—Literature.

1. Sources. The following bibliography of Manichæism is taken from Schaff's History of the Christian Church, vol. II. pp. 498–500 (new edition). Additions are indicated by brackets. 1. Oriental Sources: The most important, though of comparatively late date. (a) Mohammedan (Arabic): Kitâb al Fihrist. A history of Arabic literature to 987, by an Arab of Bagdad, usually called Ibn Abi Jakub An-Nadîm; brought to light by Flügel, and published after his death by Rödiger and Müller, in 2 vols. Leipz. 1871-'72. Book IX. section first, treats of Manichæism. Flügel's translation, see below. Kessler calls the Fihrist a "Fündstätte allerersten Ranges." Next to it comes the relation of the Mohammedan philosopher, Al-Shahrastani(d. 1153), in his History of Religious Parties and Philosophical Sects, Ed. Cureton, Lond. 1842, 2 vols. (I. 188–192); German translation by Haarbrücker, Halle, 1851. On other Mohammedan sources, see Kessler in Herzog, IX., 225 sq. (b) Persian Sources: relating to the life of Mani, the Shâhnâmeh (the King's Book) of Firdausi; ed. by Jul. Mohl, Paris, 1866 (V. 472–475). See Kessler, ibid. 225. [Albiruni's Chronology of Ancient Nations, tr. by E. Sachau, and published by the Oriental Translation Fund, Lond. 1879. Albîrunî lived 973–1048, and is said to have possessed vast literary resources no longer available to us. His work seems to be based on early Manichæan sources, and strikingly confirms the narrative preserved by the Fihrist. See also articles by Westand Thomasin Journal of the Asiatic Society, 1868, 1870, 1871.] (c) Christian Sources: In Arabic, the Alexandrian Patriarch Eutychius (d. 916). Annales, ed. Pococke, Oxon. 1628;

Barhebræus (d. 1286), in his Historia Dynastiarum, ed. Pococke. In Syriac: Ephraem Syrus (d. 393), in various writings. Esnigor Esnik, an Armenian bishop of the 5th Century, who wrote against Marcion and Mani (German translation from the Armenian by C. Fr. Neumann, in Illgen's Zeitschrift für die Hist. Theologie, 1834, pp.77–78). 2. Greek Sources: [Alexander of Lycopolis: The Tenets of the Manichæans (first published by Combefis, with a Latin version, in the Auctararium Novissimum, Bibl. S. S. Patrum; again by Gallandi, in his Bibl. Patrum, vol. IV. p. 73 sq. An English translation by Rev. James B.H. Hawkins, M .A ., appeared in Clark's Ante-Nicene Library, Vol. XIV. p. 236 sq.; Am. ed. vol. VI. p. 237 sq. Alexander represents himself as a convert from Paganism to Manichæism, and from Manichæism to Orthodoxy. He claims to have learned Manichæism from those who were intimately associated with Mani himself, and is, therefore, one of the earliest witnesses.1] Eusebius(H. E. VII. 31, a brief account). Epiphanius(Haer.66). Cyril of Jerusalem (Catech. VI. 20 sq.). Titus of Bostra (πρὸσ Μανιχαίουσ, ed P. de Lagarde, 1859). Photius: Adv. Manichæos (Cod. 179, Biblioth.). John of Damascus: De Haeres. and Dial. [Petrus Siculus, Hist. Manichæorum.]

3. Latin Sources: Archelaus (Bishop of Cascar in Mesopotamia, d. about 278): Acta Disputationis cum Manete Hæresiarcha; first written in Syriac, and so far belonging to the Oriental Christian Sources (Comp. Jerome, de Vir. Ill. 72), but extant only in a Latin translation, which seems to have been made from the Greek, edited by Zacagni (Rome, 1698), and Routh (in Reliquiæ Sacræ, vol. V. 3–206); Eng. transl. in Clark's Ante-Nicene Library (vol. XX. 272–419). [Am. ed. vol.

VI. p. 173 sq.]. These Acts purport to contain the report of a disputation between Archelaus and Mani before a large assembly, which was in full sympathy with the orthodox bishop, but (as Beausobre first proved), they are in form a fiction from the first quarter of the fourth century (about 320), by a Syrian ecclesiastic (probably of Edessa), yet based upon Manichæan documents, and containing much information about Manichæan doctrines. They consist of various pieces, and were the chief source of information to the West. Mani is represented (ch. 12), as appearing in a many-colored cloak and trousers, with a sturdy staff of ebony, a Babylonian book under his left arm, and with a mien of an old Persian master. In his defense he quotes freely from the N.T. At the end, he makes his escape to Persia (ch. 55). Comp. H. V. Zittwitz: Die Acta Archelai et Manetis untersucht, in Kahnis' Zeitschrift für d. Hist. Theol. 1873, No. IV. Oblasinski: Acta Disput. Arch., etc. Lips. 1874 (inaugural dissert.). Ad. Harnack: Die Acta Archelai und das Diatessaron Tatians, in Texte und Untersuchungen zur Gesch. der altchristl. Lit.vol. I. Heft 3 (1883), p. 137–153. Harnack tries to prove that the Gospel variations of Archelaus are taken from Tatian's Diatessaron.

St. Augustin (d. 430, the chief Latin authority next to the translation of Archelaus). [Besides the treatises published in Clark's series, Contra Fortunatum quendam Manichæorum Presbyterum Disput. I. et II., Contra Adimantum Manichæi discipulum, Contra Secundinum Manichæum, De Natura Boni, De duabus Animabus, De Utilitate Credendi, De Haeres. XLVI. Of these, De duabus Animabus, Contra Fortunatum, and De Natura Boniare added in the present edition, and De Utilitate Credendi has been included among Augustin's shorter theological treatises in vol. III. of the present series. In the Confessions and the Letters, moreover, the Manichæans figure prominently. The treatises included in the present series may be said to fairly represent Augustin's manner of dealing with Manichæism. The Anti-Manichæan writings are found chiefly in vol. VIII. of the Benedictine edition, and in volumes I. and XI. of the Migne reprint. Augustin's personal connection with the sect extending over a period of nine years, and his consummate ability in dealing with this form of error, together with the fact that he quotes largely from Manichæan literature, render his works the highest authority for Manichæism as it existed in the West at the close of the fifth century.] Comp. also the Acts of Councils against the Manichæans from the fourth century onwards, in Mansi and Hefele [and Hardouin].

II. Modern Works. Isaac de Beausobre (b. 1659 in France, pastor of the French church in Berlin, d. 1738): Histoire Crit. de Manichée et du Manichéisme, Amst. 1634 and '39, 2 vols. 4to. Part of the first volume is historical, the second doctrinal. Very full and scholarly. He intended to write a third volume on the later Manichæans. F. Chr. Baur: Das Manichäische Religionssystem nach den Quellen neu untersucht und entwickelt,Tüb. 1831 (500 pages). A comprehensive, philosophical and critical view. He calls the Manich. system a "glühend prächtiges Natur-und Weltgedicht." [An able critique of Baur's work by Schneckenburger appeared in the "Theol. Studien u. Kritiken,"1833, p. 875 sq. Schneckenburger strives to make it appear that Baur unduly minifies the Christian element in Manichæism. Later researches have tended to confirm Baur's main position. The Oriental sources employed by Flügel and Kessler have thrown much light upon the character of primitive Manichæism, and have enabled us to determine more precisely than Beausobre and Baur were able to do the constituent elements of Mani's system. A.V. Wegnern: Manichæorum Indulgentiæ, Lips. 1827. Wegnern points out the resemblance between the Manichæan system, in accordance with which the "hearers" participate in the merits of the "elect" without subjecting themselves to the rigorous asceticism practiced by the latter, and the later doctrine and practice of indulgences in the Roman Catholic church.] Trechsel: Ueber Kanon, Kritik und Exegese der Manichäer, Bern, 1832. D. Chwolson: Die Ssabier und der Ssabismus, Petersb. 1856, 2 vols. G. Flugel: Mani, seine Lehre und seine Scriften. Aus dem Fihrist des Abî Jakub an-Nadîm (987), Leipz. 1862. Text, translation and commentary, 440 pages. [Of the highest value, the principal document on which the work is based being, probably, the most authentic exposition of primitive Manichæan doctrine.] K. Kessler: Untersuchungen zur Genesis des Manich. Rel. Systems, Leipz. 1876. By the same: Mânî oder Beiträge zur Kenntniss der Religionsmischung im Semitismus, Leipz. 1887. See also his thorough article, Mânî und die Manichær, in "Herzog," new ed. vol. IX. 223–259 (abridged in Schaff's "Encyclop." II. 1396–1398). [Kessler has done more than any other writer to establish the relation between the Manichæans and the earlier Oriental sects, and between these and the old Babylonian religion. The author of this introduction wishes to express his deep obligation to Kessler. The article on the "Mandäer" in "Herzog," by the same author, is valuable in this connection, though his attempt to exclude all historical connection between this Babylonian Gnostic sect and Palestine can hardly be pronounced a success. J. B. Mozley: Ruling Ideas in Early Ages; lecture on "The Manichæans and the Jewish Fathers," with special reference to Augustin's method of dealing with the cavils of the Manichæans.] G. T. Stokes: Manes and Manichæans, in "Smith and Wace," III. 792–801. A. Harnack: Manichæism in 9th ed. of the "Encycl. Britannica," vol. XV. (1883), 481–487. [Also in German, as a Beigabe to his Lehrbuch d. Dogmengeschichte, vol. I. p. 681 sq. Harnack follows Kessler in all essential particulars. Of Kessler's article in "Herzog" he says: "This article contains the best that we possess on Manichæism." In this we concur. W. Cunningham: S. Austin and his Place in the History of Christian Thought, Hulsean Lectures, 1885, p. 45–72, and passim, Lond. 1886. This treatise is of considerable value, especially as it regards the philosophical attitude of Augustin towards Manichæism.] The accounts of Mosheim, Lardner, Schröckh, Walch, Neander, Gieseler [and Wolf].

Chapter II.—Philosophical Basis, and Antecedents of Manichæism.

"About 500 years before the commencement of the Christian era," writes Professor Monier Williams, "a great stir seems to have taken place in Indo-Aryan, as in Grecian minds, and indeed in thinking minds everywhere throughout the then civilized world. Thus when Buddha arose in India, Greece had her thinkers in Pythagoras, Persia in Zoroaster, and China in Confucius. Men began to ask themselves earnestly such questions as—What am I? Whence have I come? Whither am I going? How can

I explain my consciousness of personal existence? What is the relationship between my material and immaterial nature? What is the world in which I find myself? did a wise, good and all-powerful Being create it out of nothing? or did it evolve out of an eternal germ? or did it come together by the combination of eternal atoms? If created by a Being of infinite wisdom, how can I account for the inequality of condition in it—good and evil, happiness and misery. Has the Creator form or is he formless? Has he any qualities or none?"

It is true that such questions pressed themselves with special importunity upon the thinkers of the age mentioned, but we should be far astray if we should think for a moment that now for the first time they suggested themselves and demanded solution. The fact is that the earliest literary records of the human race bear evidence of high thinking on the fundamental problems of God, man, and the world, and the relations of these to each other. Recent scholars have brought to light facts of the utmost interest with reference to the preBabylonian (Accadian) religion. A rude nature-worship, with a pantheistic basis, but assuming a polytheistic form, seems to have prevailed in Mesopotamia from a very early period. "Spirit everywhere dispersed produced all the phenomena of nature, and directed and animated all created beings. They caused evil and good, guided the movements of the celestial bodies, brought back the seasons in their order, made the wind to blow and the rain to fall, and produced by their influence atmospheric phenomena both beneficial and destructive; they also rendered the earth fertile, and caused plants to germinate and to bear fruit, presided over the births and preserved the lives of living beings, and yet at the same time sent death and disease. There were spirits of this kind everywhere, in the starry heavens, in the earth, and in the intermediate region of the atmosphere; each element was full of them, earth, air, fire and water; and nothing could exist without them...As evil is everywhere present in nature side by side with good, plagues with favorable influences, death with life, destruction with fruitfulness; an idea of dualism as decided as in the religion of Zoroaster pervaded the conceptions of the supernatural world formed by the Accadian magicians, the evil beings of which they feared more than they valued the powers of good. There were essentially good spirits, and others equally bad. These opposing troops constituted a vast dualism, which embraced the whole universe and kept up a perpetual struggle in all parts of the creation." This primitive Turanian quasi-dualism (it was not dualism in the strictest sense of the term) was not entirely obliterated by the Cushite and Semitic civilizations and cults that successively overlaid it. So firmly rooted had this early mode of viewing the world become that it materially influenced the religions of the invaders rather than suffered extermination. In the Babylonian religion of the Semitic period the dualistic element was manifest chiefly in the magical rites of the Chaldean priests who long continued to use Accadian as their sacred language. "Upon this dualistic conception rested the whole edifice of sacred magic, of magic regarded as a holy and legitimate intercourse established by rites of divine origin, between man and the supernatural beings surrounding him on all sides. Placed unhappily amid this perpetual struggle between the good and bad spirits, man felt himself attacked by them at every moment; his fate depended upon them....He needed then some aid against the attacks of the bad spirits, against the plagues and diseases which they sent upon him. This help he hoped to find in incantations, in mysterious and powerful words, the secret of which was known only to the priests of magic, in their prescribed rites and their talismans...The Chaldeans had such a great idea of the power and efficacy of their formulæ, rites and amulets, that they came to regard them as required to fortify the good spirits themselves in their combat with the demons, and as able to give them help by providing them with invincible weapons which should ensure success." A large number of magical texts have been preserved and deciphered, and among them "the 'favorable Alad,' the 'favorable Lamma,' and the 'favorable Utuq,' are very frequently opposed...to the 'evil Alad,' the 'evil Lamma,' the 'evil Utuq.'" It would be interesting to give in detail the results of the researches of George Smith, Lenormant, A.H. Sayce, E. Schrader, Friedrich Delitzsch and others, with reference to the elaborate mythological and cosmological systems of the Babylonians. Some of the features thereof will be brought out further on by way of comparison with the Manichæan mythology and cosmology. Suffice it to say that the dualistic element is everywhere manifest, though not in so consistent and definite a form as in Zoroastrianism, to say nothing of Manichæism.

The Medo-Persian invasion brought into Babylonia the Zoroastrian system, already modified, no doubt, by the Elamitic (Cushite) cult. Yet the old Babylonian religion was too firmly rooted to be supplanted, even by the religion of such conquerors as Darius and Cyrus. Modifications, however, it undoubtedly underwent. The dualism inherent in the system became more definite. The influence of the Jews in Mesopotamia upon the ancient population cannot have been inconsiderable, especially as many of the former, including probably most of the captives of the Northern tribes, were absorbed by the latter. Because of this blending of old Babylonian, Persian, and Hebrew blood, traditions, and religious ideas, there was developed in Mesopotamia a type of religious thought that furnished a philosophical basis and a mythological and cosmological garnishing for the Manichæan system. Dualism, therefore, arising from efforts of the unaided human mind to account for the natural phenomena that appear beneficent and malignant, partly of old Babylonian origin and partly of Persian, but essentially modified by Hebrew influence more or less pure, furnished to Mani the foundation of his system. We shall attempt at a later stage of the discussion to determine more accurately the relations of Manichæism to the various systems with which correctly or incorrectly it has been associated. Suffice it to say, at present, that no new problem presented itself to Mani, and that he furnished no essentially new solution of the problems that had occupied the attention of his countrymen for more than 2500 years. Before proceeding to institute a comparison between Manichæism and the various systems of religious thought to which it stands related, it will be advantageous to have before us an exposition of the Manichæan system itself, based upon the most authentic sources.

Chapter III.—The Manichæan System. Earlier writers on Manichæism have, for the most part, made the Acta Disp. Archelai et Manetisand the anti-Manichæan writings of Augustin the basis of their representations. For later Manichæism in the West, Augustin is beyond question the highest authority, and the various polemical treatises which he put forth exhibit the system under almost every imaginable aspect. The "Acts of the Disputation of Archelaus and Manes," while it certainly rests upon a somewhat extensive and accurative knowledge of early Manichæism, is partially discredited by its generally admitted spuriousness—spuriousness in the sense that it is not a genuine record of a real debate. It is highly probable that debates of this kind occurred between Mani and various Christian leaders in the East, and so Mani may at one time or other have given utterance to most of the statements that are attributed to him in this writing; or these statements may have been derived, for substance, from his numerous treatises, and have been artfully adapted to the purposes of the writer of the "Acts." It is certain that most of the representations are correct. But we can no longer rely upon it as an authentic firsthand authority. Since Flügel published the treatise from the Fihrist entitled "The Doctrines of the Manichæans, by Muhammad ben Ishâk," with a German translation and learned annotations, it has been admitted that this treatise must be made the basis for all future representations of Manichæism. Kessler, while he has had access to many other Oriental documents bearing upon the subject, agrees with Flügel in giving the first place to this writing. On this exposition of the doctrines of the Manichæans, therefore, as expounded by Flügel and Kessler, we must chiefly rely. The highly poetical mythological form which Mani gave to his speculations renders it exceedingly difficult to arrive at assured results with reference to fundamental principles. If we attempt to state in a plain matter-of-fact way just what Mani taught we are in constant danger of misrepresenting him. In fact, one of the favorite methods employed against Mani's doctrines by the writer of the "Acts of the Disputation," etc., as well as by Augustin and others, was to reduce Mani's poetical fancies to plain language and thus to show their absurdity. The considerations which have led experts like Flügel and Kessler to put so high an estimate upon this document, and the discussions as to the original language in which the sources of the document were written, are beyond the scope of this essay. Suffice it to say, that so far as we can form a judgment on the matter, the reasons for ascribing antiquity and authenticity to the representation of Manichæism contained in the document are decisive.

1. Mani's Life. According to the Fihrist, Mani's father, a Persian by race, resided at Coche on the Tigris, about forty miles north of Babylon. Afterwards he removed into Babylonia and settled at Modein, where he frequented an idol-temple like the rest of the people. He next became associated with a party named Mugtasila (Baptizers), probably identical with or closely related to the Mandæans and Sabeans, both of which parties made much of ceremonial bathing. Mani, who was born after the removal to Babylonia, is related to have been the recipient of angelic visitations at the age of twelve. Even now he was forewarned that he must leave the religion of his father at the age of twenty-four. At the appointed time the angel At-Taum appeared again and announced to him his mission. "Hail, Mani, from me and the Lord, who has sent me to thee and chosen thee for his mission. But he commands thee to invite men to thy doctrine and to proclaim the glad tidings of truth that comes from him, and to bestow thereon all thy zeal." Mani entered upon his work, according to Flügel's careful computation, April

1, 238, or, according to calculations based on another statement, in 252. Mani maintained that he was the Paraclete promised by Jesus. He is said, in this document, to have derived his teaching from the Magi and the Christians, and the characters in which he wrote his books, from the Syriac and the Persian. After travelling in many lands for forty years and disseminating his doctrines in India, China, and Turkestan, he succeeded in impressing his views upon Fîrûz, brother of King Sapor, who had intended to put him to death. Sapor became warmly attached to Mani and granted toleration to his followers. Afterwards, according to some accounts, Mani was imprisoned by Sapor and liberated by his successor Hormizd. He is said to have been crucified by order of King Bahraîm I. (276-'7), and his skin stuffed with straw is said to have been suspended at the city gate. Eusebius (H. E. VII. 31) describes Mani as "a barbarian in life, both in speech and conduct, who attempted to form himself into a Christ, and then also proclaimed himself to be the very Paraclete and the Holy Spirit. Then, as if he had been Christ, he selected twelve disciples, the partners of his new religion, and after patching together false and ungodly doctrines collected from a thousand heresies long since extinct, he swept them off like a deadly poison from Persia, upon this part of the world." The account given in the Acta Archel (written probably about 330-'40), is far more detailed than that of the Fihrist and differs widely therefrom. It contains much that is highly improbable. Mani is represented as having for his predecessors one Scythianus, an Egyptian heretic of Apostolic times, and Terebinthus, who went with him to Palestine and after the death of Scythianus removed to Babylonia. The writings of Terebinthus or Scythianus came into the possession of a certain widow, who purchased Mani when seven years of age (then named Cubricus) and made him heir of her property and books. He changed his name to Mani (Manes), and, having become imbued with the teachings of the books, began at about sixty years of age to promulgate their teachings, choosing three disciples, Thomas, Addas and Hermas, to whom he entrusted the writings mentioned above, along with some of his own. Up to this time he knew little of Christianity, but having been imprisoned by the king for failure in a promised cure of the king's son, he studied the Christian Scriptures and derived therefrom the idea of the Paraclete, which he henceforth applied to himself. After his escape the famous dialogue with Archelaus and that with Diodorus occurred. Returning to Arabion he was arrested, carried to Persia, flayed alive, and his skin stuffed and suspended as above. Some additional facts from an Oriental source used by Beausobre have more or less verisimilitude. According to this, Mani was born of Magian parents about 240 A.D. He became skilled in music, mathematics, geography, astronomy, painting, medicine, and in the Scriptures. The account of his ascendancy over Sapor and his subsequent martyrdom is substantially the same as that of the Fihrist. Albîrunî's work (see bibliography preceding) confirms the account given by the Fihrist. The conversion of Sapor to Manichæism (in A.D.261) is said to be confirmed by Sassanian inscriptions (see Journal of Asiat. Soc. 1868 p. 310-'41, and ibid. p. 376, and 1871 p. 416).

The Fihrist's account contains a long list of the works of Mani, which is supplemented by other Oriental and Western notices. The list is interesting as showing the wide range of Mani's literary activity, or at least of the literature that was afterwards connected with his name.

2. Mani's System. As the life of Mani has been the subject of diversified and contradictory representations, so also have his doctrines. Here, too, we must make the account given by the Fihrist fundamental. It will be convenient to treat the subject under the following heads: Theology, Cosmogony, Anthropology, Soteriology, Cultus, Eschatology, and Ethics.

(1.) Theology. Mani taught dualism in the most unqualified sense. Zoroastrianism is commonly characterized as dualistic, yet it is so in no such sense as is Manichæism. According to the Fihrist, "Mani teaches: Two subsistences form the beginning of the world, the one light the other darkness; the two are separated from each other. The light is the first most glorious being, limited by no number, God himself, the King of the Paradise of Light. He has five members: meekness, knowledge, understanding, mystery, insight; and five other spiritual members: love, faith, truth, nobleness, and wisdom. He maintained furthermore that the God of light, with these his attributes, is without beginning, but with him two equally eternal things likewise exist, the one the atmosphere, the other the earth. Mani adds: and the members of the atmosphere are five [the first series of divine attributes mentioned above are enumerated]; and the members of the earth are five [the second series]. The other being is the darkness, and his members are five: cloud, burning, hot wind, poison, and darkness. Mani teaches: that the light subsistence borders immediately on the dark subsistence, without a dividing wall between them; the light touches with its (lowest) side the darkness, while upwards to the right and left it is unbounded. Even so the darkness is endless downwards and to the right and left."

This represents Mani's view of the eternally existent status quo, before the conflict began, and the endless state after the conflict ceases. What does Mani mean, when he enumerates two series of five attributes each as members of God, and straightway postulates the coeternity of atmosphere and earth and divides these self-same attributes between the latter? Doubtless Mani's theology was fundamentally pantheistic, i.e., pantheistic within the limits of each member of the dualism. The God of Light himself is apparently conceived of as transcending thought. Atmosphere and Earth (not the atmosphere and earth that we know, but ideal atmosphere and earth) are the æons derived immediately from the Ineffable One and coëternal with him. The ten attributes are æons which all belong primarily to the Supreme Being and secondarily to the two great æons, half to each. The question may arise, and has been often discussed, whether Mani meant to identify God (the Prince of Light) with the Kingdom of Light? His language, in this treatise, is wavering. He seems to struggle against such a representation, yet without complete success.

What do the other sources teach with reference to the absoluteness of the dualism and with reference to the identification of the Prince of Light with the Kingdom of Light? According to the Acts of the Disputation of Archelaus and Manes,6Manes "worships two deities, unoriginated, self-existent, eternal, opposed the one to the other. Of them he represents the one as good, and the other as evil, and assigned the name of Light to the former, and that of Darknessto the latter." Again, Manes is represented as saying: "I hold that there are two natures, one good and another evil; and that the one which is good dwells in a certain part proper to it, but that the evil one is this world as well as all things in it, which are placed there like objects imprisoned in the portion of the wicked one" (1 John 5, 19). According to Alexander of Lycopolis,7"Mani laid down two principles, God and matter (Hyle). God he called good, and matter he affirmed to be evil. But God excelled more in good than matter in evil." Alexander goes on to show how Mani used the word Hyle, comparing the Manichæan with the Platonic teaching. Statements of substantially the same purport might be multiplied. As regards the identification of God (the King of Light) with the Kingdom of Light, and of Satan (the King of Darkness) with the Kingdom of Darkness, the sensuous poetical way in which Mani expressed his doctrines may leave us in doubt. The probability is, however, that he did pantheistically identify each element of the dualism with his Kingdom. He personifies the Kingdom of Light and the Kingdom of Darkness, and peoples these Kingdoms with fanciful beings, which are to be regarded as personified attributes of the principles of darkness and light.

A word on the Manichæan conception of matter or Hylemay not be out of place in this connection. It would seem that the Manichæans practically identified Hyleor matter with the Kingdom of Darkness. At any rate Hyle is unoriginated and belongs wholly to this Kingdom.

(2.) Cosmogony. So much for the Manichæan idea of the Kingdom of Light and the Kingdom of Darkness before the great conflict that resulted in the present order of things. Why did not they remain separate? Let us learn from the Fihrist's narrative: "Mani teaches further: Out of this dark earth [the Kingdom of Darkness] arose Satan, not that he was in himself eternal from the beginning, yet were his substances in his elements unoriginated. These substances now united themselves out of his elements and went forth as Satan, his head as the head of a lion, his body as the body of a dragon, his wings as the wings of a bird, his tail as the tail of a great fish, and his four feet as the feet of creeping animals. When this Satan under the name Iblis, the (temporally considered) eternal (primeval), had arisen out of the darkness, he devoured and consumed everything, spread destruction right and left, and plunged into the deep, in all these movements bringing down from above desolation and annihilation. Then he strove for the height, and descried the beams of light; but they were opposed to him. When he saw later how exalted these were, he was terrified, shriveled up, and merged himself in his elements. Hereupon he strove anew with such violence after the height, that the land of light descried the doings of Satan and how he was bent upon murder and destruction. After they had been apprised thereof, the world of Insight learned of it, then the world of Knowledge, then the world of Mystery, then the world of Understanding, then the world of Meekness. When at last, he further teaches, the King of the Paradise of Light had also learned of it, he thought how he might suppress Satan, and, Mani adds, those hosts of his would have been mighty enough to overpower Satan. Yet he desired to do this by means of his own might. Accordingly, he produced by means of the spirit of his right hand [i.e., the Gentle Breeze], his five worlds, and his twelve elements, a creature, and this is the (temporally considered) Eternal Man [Primordial Man], and summoned him to do battle with the Darkness. But Primordial Man, Mani adds, armed himself with the five races [natures], and these are the five gods, the Gentle Breeze, the Wind, the Light, the Water and the Fire. Of them he made his armor, and the first that he put on was the Gentle Breeze. He then covered the Gentle Breeze with the burning Light as with a mantle. He drew over the Light Water filled with atoms, and covered himself with the blowing Wind. Hereupon he took the Fire as a shield and as a lance in his hand, and precipitated himself suddenly out of Paradise until he reached the border of the region that is contiguous to the battle-field. The Primordial Devil also took his five races [natures]: Smoke, Burning, Darkness, Hot Wind and Cloud; armed himself with them; made of them a shield for himself; and went to meet Primordial Man. After they had fought for a long time the Primordial Devil vanquished the Primordial Man, devoured some of his light, and surrounded him at the same time with his races and elements. Then the King of the Paradise of Light sent other gods, freed him, and vanquished the Darkness. But he who was sent by the King of Light to rescue Primordial Man is called the Friend of the Light. This one made a precipitate descent, and Primordial Man was freed from the hellish substances, along with that which he had snatched from the spirit of Darkness and which had adhered to him. When, therefore, Mani proceeds, Joyfulness and the Spirit of Life drew near to the border, they looked down into the abyss of this deep hell and saw Primordial Man and the angels [i.e., the races or natures with which he was armed], how Iblis, the Proud Oppressors, and the Dark Life surrounded them. And the Spirit of Life, says Mani, called Primordial Man with a loud voice as quick as lightning and Primordial Man became another god. When the Primordial Devil had ensnared Primordial Man in the battle, Mani further teaches, the five parts of the Light were mingled with the five parts of the Darkness."

Let us see if we can get at the meaning of this great cosmological poem as far as we have gone. The thing to be accounted for is the mixture of good and evil. The complete separation of the eternally existent Kingdoms of Light and Darkness has been posited. How now are we to account for the mixture of light and darkness, of good and evil, in the present order of things? Mani would account for it by supposing that a conflict had occurred between an insufficiently equipped representative of the King of Light and the fully equipped ruler of the Kingdom of Darkness. His view of the vastly superior power of the King of Light would not allow him to suppose that the King of Light fully equipped had personally contended with the King of Darkness, and suffered the loss and contamination of his elements. Yet he only clumsily obviates this difficulty; for Primordial Man is produced and equipped by the King of Light for the very purpose of combating the King of Darkness, and Mani saves the King of Light from personal contamination only by impugning his judgment.

We have now reached the point where, because of the conflict, good and evil are blended. We must beware of supposing that Mani meant to ascribe any kind of materiality to the members of the Kingdom of Light. The Kingdom of Light, on the contrary, he regarded as purely spiritual; the Kingdom of Darkness as material. We have now the conditions for the creation of the present order of things, including man. How does Mani picture the process and the results of this mixing of the elements?

"The smoke (or vapor) was mingled with the gentle breeze (zephyr), and the present atmosphere resulted. So that whatever of agreeableness and power to quicken the soul and animal life is found in it [resultant air], is from the zephyr, and whatever of destructiveness and noisomeness is found in it, proceeds from the smoke. The burning was mingled with the fire; therefore whatever of conflagration, destruction and ruin is found, is from the burning, but whatever of brightness and illumination is in it [the resultant fire], springs from the fire. The light mingled itself with the darkness; therefore in dense bodies as gold, silver and the like, whatever of brightness, beauty, purity and other useful qualities occurs, is from the light, and whatever of tarnish, impurity, density and hardness occurs, springs from the darkness. The hot wind was mingled with the wind; whatever now is useful and agreeable in this [resultant wind] springs from the wind, and whatever of uneasiness, hurtfulness and deleterious property is found in it [resultant wind] is from the hot wind. Finally, the mist was mingled with the water, so that what is found in this [resultant water] of clearness, sweetness, and soul-satisfying property, is from the water; whatever, on the contrary, of overwhelming, suffocating, and destroying power, of heaviness, and corruption, is found in it, springs from the mist."

But we must from this point abbreviate the somewhat prolix account. Primordial Man, after the blending of the elements, ascended on high accompanied by "one of the angels of this intermingling;" in other words, snatching away a part of the imprisoned elements of the Kingdom of Light.

The next step is the creation of the present world, which Mani ascribes to the King of the World of Light, the object being to provide for the escape of the imprisoned elements of Light. Through an angel he constructed ten heavens and eight earths, an angel being appointed to hold heavens and earths in their places. A description of the stairways, doors, and halls of the heavens is given in the Fihrist's narrative. The stairways lead to the "height of heaven." The air was used as a medium for connecting heaven and earth. A pit was formed to be the receptacle of darkness from which the light should be liberated. The sun and the moon were created to be the receptacles of the light that should be liberated from the darkness, the sun for light that has been mingled with "hot devils," the moon for that which had been mingled with "cold devils." The moon is represented as collecting light during the first half-month, and during the second pouring it into the sun. When the sun and moon have liberated all the light they are able, there will be a fire kindled on the earth which will burn for 1468 years, when there will be no light left. The King of Darkness and his hosts will thereupon withdraw into the pit prepared for them.

(3.) Anthropology. So much for the liberation of the imprisoned light, which, according to Mani, was the sole object of creation. As yet we have heard nothing of the creation of living creatures. What place do man, the lower animals, and plants sustain in the Manichæan economy? We are to keep constantly in mind that Primordial Man was not Adam, but a divine æon, and that he ascended into the heights immediately after the blending of parts of his armor with darkness. The creation of earthly man was an altogether different affair. We must give the account of man's creation in Mani's own words, as preserved by the Fihrist: "Hereupon one of those Arch-fiends and [one] of the Stars, and

St. Augustine

Overmastering Violence, Avarice, Lust, and Sin, copulated, and from their copulation sprang the first man, who is Adam, two Arch-fiends, a male and a female, directing the process. A second copulation followed and from this sprang the beautiful woman who is Eve."

Man, therefore, unlike the world, is the creature of demons, the aim of the demons being to imprison in man, through the propagation of the race, as much as possible of the light, and so to hinder the separating process by the sun and the moon. Avarice is represented as having secretly seized some of the divine light and imprisoned it in man. The part played by the Star in the production of man is somewhat obscure in the narrative, yet the Star could hardly have been regarded as wholly evil. Probably the Star was thought of as a detached portion of the light that had not entered into the sun or the moon. "When, therefore, the five Angels saw what had taken place, they besought the Messenger of Joyful Knowledge, the Mother of Life, Primordial Man and the Spirit of Life, to send someone to liberate and save man, to reveal to him knowledge and righteousness, and to free him from the power of the devils. They sent, accordingly, Jesus, whom a god accompanied. These seized the two Arch-fiends, imprisoned them and freed the two creatures (Adam and Eve.)"

Jesus warned Adam of Eve's violent importunity, and Adam obeyed his injunction not to go near her. One of the Arch-fiends, however, begat with her a son named Cain, who in turn begat Abel of his mother, and afterwards two maidens Worldly wise and Daughter-of Avarice. Cain took the first to wife and gave the other to Abel. An angel having begotten of Worldly-wise two beautiful daughters (Raufarjâd and Barfarjâd), Abel accused Cain of the act. Cain enraged by the false accusation slew Abel and took Worldly-wise to wife. So far Adam had kept himself pure, but Eve was instructed by a demon in the art of enchanting, and she was enabled to excite his lust and to entrap him. By Adam she bore a beautiful son, whom the demon urged Eve to destroy. Adam stole the child away and brought it up on cow's milk and fruit. This son was named Seth (Schatil). Adam once more yielded to Eve's fascinations, but through Seth's exhortations was induced to flee "eastward to the light and the wisdom of God." Adam, Seth, Raufarjâd, Barfarjâd, and Worldly-wise died and went to Paradise; while Eve, Cain, and Daughter-of-Avarice went into Hell. This fantastic perversion of the Biblical narrative of the creation and fall of man has many parallels in Rabbinic literature, and doubtless Mani first became acquainted with the narrative in a corrupted form. The teaching, however, of this mythologizing evidently is that the indulgence of the flesh and the begetting of children furnish the chief obstacle to the separation of light from darkness. Adam is represented as striving to escape from the allurements of Eve, but Eve is aided by demonic craft in overcoming him. Yet Adam does not become enslaved to lust, and so at last is saved. Eve, lustful from the beginning, is lost along with those of like disposition.

(4.) Soteriology. Such was, apparently, Mani's conception of the creation of man, and of the attempts to liberate the light that was in him. What were his practical teachings to men of his time as to the means of escape from the Kingdom of Darkness into the Kingdom of Light? What view did Mani take of the historical Jesus? The Jesus who warned Adam against the seductions of Eve was evidently not the Jesus of the New Testament.

According to the narrative of the Fihrist, Mani "maintained that Jesus is a devil." Such a statement occurs nowhere else, so far as we are aware, in the literature of Manichæism. The sources, however, are unanimous in ascribing to Mani a completely docetical view of the person of Christ. In using this blasphemous language, he probably referred to the representations of Jesus as God manifest in the flesh, which he regarded as Jewish and abominable. The New Testament narratives Mani [or at least his followers] regarded as interpolated in the interest of Judaism. Later Manichæans, under the influence of Marcionism (and orthodoxy) gave to Jesus a far more prominent place in the economy of man's salvation than did Mani himself.

How then is man to be saved according to Mani? It is by rigorous asceticism, and by the practice of certain ceremonial observances. Mani does not rise above the plane of ordinary heathenism in his plan of salvation. "It is incumbent upon him who will enter into the religion that he prove himself, and that if he sees that he is able to subdue lust and avarice, to leave off the eating of all kinds of flesh, the drinking of wine, and connubial intercourse, and to withhold himself from what is injurious in water, fire, magic and hypocrisy, he may enter into the religion; but if not let him abstain from entering. But if he loves religion, yet is not able to repress sensuality and avarice, yet he may make himself serviceable for the maintenance of religion and of the Truthful [i.e.the 'Elect'], and may meet (offset) his corrupt deeds through the use of opportunities where he wholly gives himself up to activity, righteousness, zealous watchfulness, prayer and pious humiliation; for this suffices him in this transitory world and in the future eternal world, and his form in the last day will be the second form, of which, God willing, we shall treat further below."

The doctrine of indulgences of which the germs appeared in the Catholic church even before the time of Mani, is here seen fully developed. What the Greek and Latin sources call the Elector Perfect and the Hearers, are undoubtedly indicated here by those who can devote themselves to rigidly ascetical living, and those who, without such qualifications, are willing to exert themselves fully on behalf of the cause. These latter evidently become partakers of the merits of those who carry out the ascetical regulations. That this is primitive Manichæan doctrine is abundantly proved by the general agreement of ancient writers of all classes. It is noteworthy that nothing Christian appears among the conditions of Manichæan discipleship. It is not faith in Christ, but the ability to follow a particular kind of outward life that confers standing in the Manichæan society.

(5.) Cultus. Let us next look at the precepts of Mani to the initiated: "Mani imposed upon his disciples commandments, namely, ten commandments, and to these are attached three seals, and fasts of seven days in each month. The commandments are: Faith in the four most glorious essences: God, his Light, his Power, and his Wisdom. But God, whose name is glorious, is the King of the Paradise of Light; his Light is the sun and the moon, his Power the five angels: Gentle Breeze, Wind, Light, Water and Fire; and his Wisdom the Sacred Religion. This embraces five ideas: that of teachers, the sons of Meekness; that of those enlightened by the Sun, sons of Knowledge; that of the presbyters, sons of Reason; that of the Truthful, sons of Mystery; that of exposition of the doctrines of the Manichæans by quoting from the Fihrist Mani's teachings on eschatology.

"When death approaches a Truthful One ('Elect'), teaches Mani, Primordial Man sends a Light-God in the form of a guiding Wise One, and with him three gods, and along with these the water-vessel, clothing, head-gear, crown, and garland of light. With them comes the maiden, like the soul of this Truthful One. There appears to him also the devil of avarice and lust, along with other devils. As soon as the Truthful Man sees these he calls the goddess who has assumed the form of the Wise One and the three other gods to his help, and they draw near him. As soon as the devils are aware of their presence they turn and flee. The former, however, take this Truthful One, clothe him with the crown, the garland and the robe, put the water-vessel in his hand and mount with him upon the pillars of promise to the sphere of the moon, to Primordial Man, and to Nahnaha, the Mother of the Living, to the position in which he was at first in the Paradise of Light. But his body remains lying as before in order that the sun, the moon, and the gods of Light may withdraw from it the powers, i.e., the water, the fire and the gentle breeze, and he rises to the sun and becomes a god. But the rest of his body, which is wholly darkness, is cast into hell."

In the case of Manichæans of the lower order, described above, the same divine personages appear at his summons. "They free him also from devils, but he ceases not to be like a man in the world, who in his dreams sees frightful forms and sinks into filth and mire. In this condition he remains, until his light and his spirit are liberated and he has attained to the place of union with the Truthful, and after a long period of wandering to and fro puts on their garments."

To the sinful man, on the other hand, the divine personages appear, not to free him from the devils that are tormenting him, but rather to "overwhelm him with reproaches, to remind him of his deeds, and strikingly to convince him that he has renounced help for himself, from the side of the Truthful. Then wanders he round about in the world, unceasingly chased by torments, until this order of things ceases, and along with the world he is cast into hell."

There is nothing original about the eschatology of Mani, and scarcely anything Christian. We see in it a fully developed doctrine of purgatory, somewhat like the Platonic, and still more like that of the later Catholic church. Salvation consists simply in the liberation of the light from the darkness. In the case of the Elect this takes place immediately after death; in the case of adherents who have not practiced the prescribed forms of asceticism, it takes place only after considerable torment. In the case of the ordinary sensual man, there is no deliverance. Doubtless Mani would have held that in his case, too, whatever particles of light may have been involved in his animal structure are liberated from the dead body.

(7.) Ethics. About ceremonies we find little that enlightens us in the Fihrist's account. Water (that is, water apart from the deleterious elements that have become blended with it) was regarded by Mani as one of the divine elements. The ablutions in running water mentioned above regarding the prayers may have sustained some relation to baptism, but can hardly be ascribed to Christian influence. The connection of the Manichæans with the Mandæans, who made much of ceremonial bathing, will be considered below. It is certain that Mani's father was connected with a baptizing party, viz., the Mugtasilah. According to the Fihrist Mani was the author of an Epistle on Baptism. The question whether Mani and his followers practiced water-baptism or not is by no means an easy one to solve. The passage cited by Giesseler from Augustin to prove that the "Elect" were initiated by baptism is inconclusive. Augustin acknowledges that God and the Manichæans themselves alone know what takes place in the secret meetings of the "Elect." Whatever ceremonies they performed, whether baptism or the Lord's supper, or some other, were matters of profound secrecy, and so we need not wonder at the lack of definite information. From a passage quoted by Augustin in his report of a discussion with Felix the Manichæan, we should certainly infer that both ordinances were practiced in some form by the Manichæans of the West. But Augustin himself says that Manichæans deny the saving efficacy of baptism, maintain that it is superfluous, do not require it of those whom they win to their views, etc. It is certain, therefore, that if they practiced baptism and the Lord's supper at all, they attached to it a meaning radically different from that of Augustin. It is possible that a ceremonial anointing with oil took the place of baptism. (Baur, p. 277 sq.). Augustin mentions a disgusting ceremony in which human semen was partaken of by the Elect in order to deliver the imprisoned light contained therein (De Haeres. 46), and he calls this ceremony a sort of Eucharist. But his confessed ignorance of the doings of the "Elect" discredits in some measure this accusation.

The Fihrist gives us no definite information about the three signacula. The seals (not signs) of the mouth, the hand (or hands), and of the bosom. In these are contained symbolically the Manichæan moral system. In the book Sadder (Hyde, p. 492) we read: "It is taught [by the Manichæans] to abstain from every sin, to eliminate every sin from hand, and tongue and thought." Augustin explains the signacula more fully and represents the Manichæans as attaching great importance to them: "When I name the mouth, I mean all the senses that are in the head; when I name the hand I mean every operation; when I name the bosom I mean every seminal lust."

It is confidently believed that the foregoing account of the Manichæan system, based upon the Arabic narratives preserved by the Fihrist, supplemented by the principal Eastern and Western sources, contains the essential facts with reference to this strange system of religious thought. Our next task will to be to ascertain, as precisely as possible, the relations that Manichæism sustained to the various religious systems with which it has commonly been associated.

Chapter IV.—Relation of Manichæism to Zoroastrianism.

The very close connection of these two systems has commonly been presupposed, and is undeniable. In fact, Manichæism has frequently been represented as Zoroastrian dualism, slightly modified by contact with Christianity and other systems. No one could possibly gain even a superficial view of the two systems without being strongly impressed with their points of resemblance. A closer examination, however, will reveal points of antagonism just as striking, and will enable us to account for the fact that Mani was put to death by a zealous Zoroastrian ruler because his recognized hostility to the state religion. The leading features of the Manichæan system are already before us. Instead of quoting at length from the Zend-Avesta, which is now happily accessible in an excellent English translation, we may for the sake of brevity quote Tiele's description of Zoroastrian dualism as a basis of comparison:

"Parsism is decidedly dualistic, not in the sense of accepting two hostile deities, for it recognizes no worship of evil beings, and teaches the adoration only of Ahura Mazda and the spirits subject to him; but in the sense of placing in hostility to each other two sharply divided kingdoms, that of light, of truth, and of purity, and that of darkness, of falsehood, and of impurity. This division is carried through the whole creation, organic and inorganic, material and spiritual. Above, in the highest sphere, is the domain of the undisputed sovereignty of the All-wise God; beneath, in the lowest abyss, the kingdom of his mighty adversary; midway between the two lies this world, the theatre of the contest.... This dualism further dominates the cosmogony, the cultus, and the entire view of the moral order of the world held by the Mazda worshippers. Not only does Anro-Maînyus (Ahriman) spoil by his counter-creations all the good creations of Ahura-Mazda (Ormuzd), but by slaying the protoplasts of man and beast, he brings death into the world, seduces the first pair to sin, and also brings forth noxious animals and plants. Man finds himself, in consequence, surrounded on all sides by the works of the spirits of darkness and by his hosts. It is the object of worship to secure the pious against their influence."

Let us bring in review some of the points of resemblance between the two systems. Both are in a sense dualistic. In both the kingdoms of Light and Darkness are set over against each other in the sharpest antagonism. In both we have similar emanations from these kingdoms (or kings). Yet, while in the Manichæan system the dualism is absolute and eternal, in the later Zoroastrian system (as in the Jewish and Christian doctrine of Satan), Ahriman (Satan) if not merely a fallen creature of Ormuzd (the good and supreme God) was at least an immeasurably inferior being. The supreme control of the universe, to which it owes its perfect order, was ascribed by Zoroastrianism to Ormuzd. The struggle between good and evil, beneficent and malevolent, was due to the opposition of the mighty, but not almighty, Ahriman. Whatever form of Mazdeism (Zoroastrianism) we take for purposes of comparison, we are safe in saying that the Manichæan dualism was by far the more absolute.

In both systems each side of the dualism is represented by a series (or rather several series) of personified principles. These agree in the two systems in some particulars. Yet the variations are quite as noticeable as the agreements. There is much in common between the Manichæan and the Zoroastrian delineations of the fearful conflict between the Kingdom of Light and the Kingdom of Darkness, yet the beginning of the conflict is quite differently conceived of in the two systems. In Manichæism the creation is accounted for by the conflict in which Primordial Man was beaten by the powers of Darkness and suffered the mixing of his elements with the elements of darkness. The actual world was made by the good God, or rather by his subordinates, as a means of liberating the imprisoned light. The creation of man is ascribed, on the other hand, to the King of Darkness (or his subordinates), with a view to hindering the escape of the mingled light by diffusion thereof through propagation. Mazdeism derives the creation solely from Ormuzd, from whose hand it issued "as pure and perfect as himself" (Lenormant, Anc. Hist. II. p. 30). It was the work of Ahriman to "spoil it by his evil influence." The appellation "Maker of the material world" is constantly applied to Ormuzd in the Vendîdâd and other sacred books. The most instructive Mazdean account of the creation that has come down to us is that contained in the Vendîdâd, Fargard I. Ahura Mazda (Ormuzd) is represented here as naming one by one the sixteen good lands that he had created. Angra Mainyu (Ahriman) is represented as coming to each, one by one, and creating in it noxious things. Examples of these counter-creations are, the serpents, winter, venomous flies, sinful lusts, mosquitoes, pride, unnatural sin, burying the dead, witchcraft, the sin of unbelief, the burning of corpses, abnormal issues in women, oppression of foreign rulers, excessive heat, etc. This jumble of physical evils and sins is characteristic of Mazdeism.

According to Mani matter is inherently evil, and it only ceases to be absolutely evil by the mixture with it of the elements of the Kingdom of Light. Creation is a process forced upon the King of Light by the ravages of the King of Darkness, and is at best only partially good. Zoroastrianism looked upon earth, fire, water, as sacred elements, to defile which was sin of the most heinous kind. Manichæism regarded actual fire and water as made up of a mixture of elements of light and darkness, and so, as by no means wholly pure. Manichæans regarded earth, so far as it consisted of dead matter, with the utmost contempt. The life-giving light in it was alone thought of with respect. Zoroastrianism somewhat arbitrarily divided animals and plants between the kingdoms of Ormuzd and Ahriman; but the idea that all material things, so far as they are material, are evil, seems never to have occurred to the early Mazdeists. Manichæans agreed with Mazdeists in their veneration for the sun, but the principles underlying this veneration seem to have been widely different in the two cases. The most radical opposition of the two systems is seen in their views of human propagation. Mani regarded the procreation of children as ministering directly to the designs of the King of Darkness to imprison the light, and so absolutely condemned it. The ZendAvestasays: (Vendîdâd, Fargard IV.): "Verily I say unto thee, O Spitama Zarathustra; the man who has a wife is far above him who begets no sons; he who keeps a house is far above him who has none; he who has children is far above a childless man." Mani made great merit of voluntary poverty. The Zend-Avesta (ibid.) says: "He who has riches is far above him who has none." Mani forbade the use of animal food as preventing the escape of the light contained in the bodies of animals. The Zend-Avesta (ibid.): "And of two men, he who fills himself with meat is filled with the good spirit much more than he who does not do so; the latter is all but dead; the former is above him by the worth of an Asperena, by the worth of a sheep, by the worth of an ox, by the worth of a man."

The eschatology of the two systems might be shown to present just as striking contrasts, and just as marked resemblances. In both systems the consummation of the age is effected by means of a conflagration, the aim of the conflagration in Mazdeism being the punishment and the purging of wicked men, the destruction of wicked spirits, the renovation of the earth, and the inauguration of the sole sovereignty of Ormuzd, while in Manichæism the aim of the conflagration is to liberate the portions of light which the processes of animal and vegetable growth, with the aid of sun and the moon have proved unable to liberate.

But enough has been said to make it evident that Manichæism was by no means a slightly altered edition of Zoroastrianism. The points of similarity between the two are certainly more apparent than real, though the historical relationship can by no means be denied.

Chapter V.—The Relation of Manichæism to the Old Babylonian Religion as Seen in Mandæism and Sabeanism.

It would have been strange indeed if the old Babylonian religion, after dominating the minds of the inhabitants of Mesopotamia for so many centuries, had given place completely to the religion of the Medo-Persian conquerors of the country. Magism itself was a mixture of old Babylonian, Medic and Persian elements. But there is much reason for believing that the primitive Babylonian faith, in a more or less pure form, persisted until long after the time of Mani, nay, that it has maintained its ground even till the present day. The researches of Chwolson, Nöldeke, Kessler and others, in the literature and history of the Mandæans and the Sabeans, combined in the last case at least with accurate knowledge of old Babylonian literature and religion, have rendered it highly probable that representatives of the old Babylonian faith were numerous in Mesopotomia and the adjoining regions at the time of Mani, and that Mani himself was more or less closely connected with it. The Mandæans were a Gnostic sect of the Ophitic type, without Christian elements. It is the opinion of Kessler, who has devoted much attention to this sect and to the relations of occult religious matters in general in Mesopotomia, that "the source of all Gnosis, and especially the immediate source of Ophitic Gnosis, is not the doctrine of the Persian Zoroaster, not Phœnicean heathenism, not the theory and practice of Greek mysteries, but the old Babylonian Chaldaic national religion, which maintained itself in Mesopotomia and Babylonia, the abode of the Ophites, Perates, Mandæans, until the post-Christian centuries, and was now opposed by the Gentiles in a mystical-ascetical form to Christianity." The close connection of the Mandæans with the Ophites, and of both with the old Babylonian religion, would seem to be established beyond question. The relation of Manichæism to Mandæism has been by no means so clearly shown. Let us look at some of the supposed points of contact. Mani's connection with the Mugtasilah sect (or Baptizers) has already been mentioned. Kessler seeks to identify this party with the Mandæans, or at least to establish a community of origin and of fundamental principles in the two parties. He would connect with the old Babylonian sect, of which ceremonial baptism seems to have been a common characteristic, the Palestinian Hemero-baptists, Elkesaites, Nazareans, Ebionites, etc. There is nothing improbable about this supposition. Certainly, we find elements in Palestinian heresy during the early Christian centuries, which we can hardly supposed to have been indigenous. And there is no more likely source of occult religious influence than Babylonia, unless it be Egypt, and there is much reason for supposing that even in Alexandria Babylonian influences were active before and after the beginning of the Christian era. Besides, many Gnostic elements different from these can be traced to Egypt. How far the Mandæans of modern times, and as they are described in extant literature, correspond with representatives of the old Babylonian religion in the third century, cannot be determined with complete certainty. Yet there is much about this party that has a primitive appearance, and the tenacity with which it has held aloof from Judaism, Manichæism, Mohammedanism, and Oriental Christianity, during centuries of conflict and oppression, says much for its conservatism. It would extend this chapter unduly to describe the elaborate cosmogony, mythology, hierarchy, ceremonial, etc., of this interesting party. For the illustration of Christian Gnosticism, the facts that have been brought out are of the utmost value. As compared with Manichæism, there is a remarkable parallelism between the two kingdoms and their subordinates or æons; the conflict between Primordial Man and the King of Darkness has its counterpart in Mandæism. The close connection of the Mandæan and the Manichæan cosmogony, together with similar views about water in the two parties, would make it highly probable that the Manichæans, like the Mandæans, practiced some kind of ceremonial ablutions.

What, now, are the grounds on which the connection of these systems with the old Babylonian religion is based? The dualistic element in the old Babylonian system was pointed out above. Kessler seeks to establish an almost complete parallelism between the Mandæan and Manichæan cosmological and mythological systems on the one hand, and the old Babylonian on the other. That there are points of striking resemblance it is certain. There is ground to suspect, however, that he has been led by partiality for a theory of his own to minimize unduly the Zoroastrian and Buddhist influence and to magnify unduly the old Babylonian. Be that as it may, there remains an important residuum of solid fact which must be taken account of by all future students of Manichæism. There is reason to hope that future work along the lines of Kessler's researches will bring to light much additional material.

Chapter VI.— The Relation of Manichæism to Buddhism.

The extent of Mani's dependence on Buddhism is a matter that has been much disputed. The attention of scholars was first directed to this possible source of Manichæism by the discovery of important features that are radically opposed to Zoroastrianism, Judaism and Christianity, and by the traditional historical connection of Mani with India and Turkestan. The antagonism of spirit and matter, of light and darkness, the mixture of spirit and light with matter and darkness in the formation of the world, the final catastrophe in which complete simplicity shall be re-established, only inert matter and darkness remaining to represent the Kingdom of Darkness, abstinence from bloody sacrifices, from marriage, from killing or eating animals—points in which Manichæism differs widely from the other systems with which it stands historically related—find their counterpart in Buddhism. It is certain, moreover, that they were fully developed in Buddhism centuries before the time of Mani. Baur, though not the first to suggest a connection of the two systems, was the first to show by a somewhat detailed comparison the close parallelism that exists between Manichæism and Buddhism. Baur's reasonings were still further elaborated and confirmed by Neander. External grounds in favor of Mani's dependence on Buddhism are the traditions of Mani's journey to India and China, and of his prolonged stay in Turkestan, where Buddhism flourished at that time. But it is on internal grounds that we chiefly rely.

If space permitted we could illustrate the close parallelism that undoubtedly exists between Manichæism and Buddhism, from Buddhist documents which have been made accessible through Professor Max Müller and his collaborators in The Sacred Book of the East, far more completely than was possible to Baur and Neander. It is certain that parallels can be found in Buddhism for almost every feature of Manichæism that is sharply antagonistic to Zoroastrianism. The Buddhist view of matter as antagonistic to spirit is fundamental. It is the world of matter that deludes. It is the body and its passions that prevent the longed for Nirvana. Buddhist asceticism is the direct outgrowth of the doctrine of the evil and delusive nature of matter. The Buddhist doctrine of metempsychosis has its precise counterpart in Manichæism, but it should be said that this doctrine was widely diffused in the West, through Pythagoreanism, before the time of Mani. The Buddhist tenderness for animal and plant life is paralleled by the Manichæan. But there is considerable difference between the views on which this tenderness is based. The Buddhist feeling was based, in part at least, upon the doctrine of metempsychosis, animals and plants being regarded as the abodes of human spirits awaiting their release into

Nirvana. The Manichæan looked upon the elements of light (life) contained in animals and plants as particles of God, and any injury done to them as a hindrance to the escape of these elements, to be conveyed away into the Kingdom of Light. Both looked upon sexual intercourse as among the greatest of evils, though the theory in the two cases was slightly different. So of the drinking of wine, the eating of animal food, etc. The final state was conceived of in substantially the same way in the two systems. Nirvana, the blowing out of man's life as an individual entity, is quite paralleled by the Manichæan view of the gradual escape of the imprisoned particles of light into the Kingdom of Light. In both cases the divine pleromais to be restored in such a way as to destroy individual consciousness.

The Buddhist Bhikkhus (or ascetical monks) correspond very closely with the Manichæan Truthful Ones (Elect), and the relations of these to ordinary adherents of the parties was much the same in the two cases. Both systems (like Christianity) had the proselyting spirit fully developed. The position of Mani as a preacher or prophet corresponds with the Buddhist idea of the manifestations of Buddha. The statement is attributed to Mani that "as Buddha came in the land of India, Zoroaster in the land of Persia, and Jesus in the land of the West, so at last in the epoch of the present this preaching came through me [Mani] in the land of Babylonia." In the interest of his theory, which makes the old Babylonian religion the chief source of Manichæism, Kessler has attempted to detract from the significance of the Buddhist influence. Yet he grants that the morality of the Manichæans (including many of the features mentioned above) was Buddhist. The close connection of the two systems cannot, it would seem, be successfully gainsaid.

Chapter VII.—The Relation of Manichæism to Judaism.

So far as a relation existed it was one of the intensest hostility. Like the Gnostics in general, Manichæism looked upon the God of the Old Testament as an evil, or at least imperfect being. On this matter we do not learn so much from the Oriental as from the Western sources, but even from the former the radical antagonism is manifest.

The statement in the Fihrist's narrative, that "Mani treated all the prophets disparagingly in his books, degraded them, accused them of lying, and maintained that devils had possessed them and that these spoke out of their mouths; nay, he goes so far as expressly to assert in some passages of his books that the prophets were themselves devils," is precisely in the line of the later Manichæan polemics against the Judaistic element in Christianity.

The Manichæan account of the creation shows some acquaintance with the Jewish Scriptures or with Jewish tradition, yet the complete perversion of the Biblical account is one of the clearest indications of hostility. It may be said in general that it is impossible to conceive of two systems of religion that have less in common, or more that is sharply antagonistic. One of the principal points of controversy between Manichæans and Christians was the defense of the Jewish Scriptures and religion by the latter. The Manichæan demanded the elimination from the current Christianity, and from the

New Testament itself, of every vestige of Judaism. Their objections to the Old Testament Scriptures and religion were in general substantially the same as those made by other Gnostics, especially by the Marcionites. The Old Testament anthropomorphic representations seem to have been offensive to them, notwithstanding their own crude conceptions of the conflict between light and darkness, of the creation, etc. The relation of God to the conquest of Canaan is a point that those inclined to cavil have never failed to make the most of. The Old Testament encouragement of race propagation, the narratives of polygamy as practiced by those that enjoyed the favor of the God of the Old Testament, the seeming approval of prevarication in several well-known cases, the institution of animal sacrifices, the allowing of the use of animal food, were among the standard objections that they raised against Judaism and against Christians who accepted the Old Testament. Judaism had, since the captivity, had many representatives in Mesopotamia, and Mani was doubtless brought up to abominate the Jews. Some of his extreme positions may have been primarily due to his radical anti-Judaistic tendencies. We shall see hereafter how Augustin met the Manichæan objections to the Old Testament.

Chapter VIII.—The Relation of Manichæism to Christianity.

Far more superficial are the relations of Manichæism to Christianity than to any of the heathen systems to which we have adverted. In fact, no Christian idea has been introduced into the system without being completely perverted. If Christian language is used, it is utterly emptied of its meaning. If Christian practices are introduced, a completely different motive lies at the basis. Indeed, the wildest of the Christian Gnostic systems kept immeasurably nearer to historical Christianity than did the Manichæans. While he blasphemed against the historical Jesus, Mani claimed to believe in Christ, a purely spiritual and divine manifestation, whose teachings had been sadly perverted by the Jews. It is scarcely possible to determine with any certainty what view Mani actually took of New Testament history. That he claimed to be a follower of Christ, and the Paraclete whom Christ had promised to send, or at least the organ of the Paraclete, Eastern and Western authorities agree. Mani is said, by Augustin, to have begun his Fundamental Epistleas follows: "Manichæus, an Apostle of Jesus Christ, by the providence of God the Father. These are wholesome words from the perennial and living fountain." So also in the Act. Archel., Mani is represented as introducing a letter: "Manichæus, an Apostle of Jesus Christ, and all the saints who are with me, and the virgins, to Marcellus, my beloved son: Grace, mercy, and peace be with you from God the Father, and from our Lord Jesus Christ." There can be no doubt but that Mani and his followers, whether from designed imposture or from less sinister motives, attempted to palm themselves off as Christians, nay, as the only true Christians. It is certain, moreover, that in this guise they gained many proselytes from the Christian ranks. As previously remarked, Mani and his followers professed to accept the New Testament Scriptures, yet they treated them in a purely subjective manner, eliminating as Judaistic interpolation whatever they could not reconcile with their own tenets. Their adherence to the New Testament, as well as their adherence to Christ, was, therefore, virtually a mere pretense. In common with Christianity, Manichæism laid much stress on redemption, yet there was nothing in common between the Christian idea of redemption through the atoning suffering of Jesus Christ and the Manichæan notion of redemption through the escape of imprisoned light. Manichæans and Christians were at one in advocating self-denial and the due subordination of the flesh. It need not be pointed out how radically different the Christian view was from the Manichæan view, already expounded. Yet pagan ascetical ideas had already invaded the Church long before the time of Mani, and many Christians were able to be attracted strongly by the Manichæan theory and practice. The later asceticism as it appeared in the hermit life of the fourth and following centuries was essentially pagan and had much in common with the Manichæan. Still more manifest is the antagonism between Manichæism and Christianity on the great fundamental principles of religion. The Manichæan and Christian ideas of God are mutually contradictory. Christianity holds fast at the same time to the unity, the omnipotence, the omniscience, the perfect wisdom, the holiness and the goodness of God. If He permits sin to exist in the world it is not because He looks upon it with complacency, nor because He lacked wisdom to provide against its rise or power to annihilate it at once when it appeared, nor because He did not foresee its rise and its ravages, but because the permission of sin forms part of His all-wise plan for the education of moral and spiritual beings. If the forces of nature are under certain circumstances hurtful or destructive to man, Christianity does not regard them as the operations of a malevolent power thwarting God's purposes, but it sees underneath the destructive violence purposes of goodness and of grace; or if it fails to see them in any given instance it yet believes that God doeth all things well. Christianity admits the existence of evil in men and in demons, yet of evil that ministers to the purposes of the Most High. Christianity is the only religion that has been able to arrive at a perfectly satisfactory theology, cosmology, anthropology, and eschatology, and this is because Christianity alone has a true and satisfying soteriology. It is God manifest in the flesh that meets all the conditions for the solution of the problem of human existence. Manichæism openly antagonized Christianity in its adherence to Old Testament revelation, including the Jewish and Christian monotheism. The good God could not, they maintained, be the creator of this world and of the universe of being. That God should be looked upon as in any sense the creator of the devil and his angels, and of the material world, was in their view an absurdity—a monstrosity. The unchristian character of the Manichæan view of matter, leading to unchristian asceticism, has already been sufficiently indicated. The reader will only need to compare the principles and practices of Manichæism, as delineated above, with those of Christianity as they are delineated in the New Testament and in the evangelical churches of to-day, to be impressed with the completely anti-Christian character of the former.

How then, it may well be asked, could Manichæism succeed as it did in fascinating so many intelligent members of the Catholic Church during the third, fourth and fifth centuries? In attempting to answer this question it should be premised that the later Western Manichæism took far more account of historical

Christianity than did Mani and his immediate followers. In the West, at least, Manichæism set itself up as the only genuine exponent of Christianity. The Jewish-Alexandrian philosophy, and Gnosticism its product, had done much towards discrediting the Old Testament Scriptures, and the moral and religious teachings therein contained. Devout Jewish and Christian thinkers who had adopted this mode of thought, had attempted by means of the allegorical method of interpretation to reconcile the seeming antagonism between Judaism and philosophy. But the process was so forced that its results could not be expected to satisfy those that felt no special interest in the removal of the difficulties. Marcionism represents a stern refusal to apply the allegory, and a determination to exhibit the antagonism between Judaism and current thought, and especially the seeming antagonism between Judaism and Christianity, in the harshest manner. Marcionism was still vigorous in the East when Manichæism arose, and through this party unfavorable views of the Old Testament were widely disseminated. Many Christians doubtless felt that the Old Testament and its religion were burdensome and trammeling to Christianity. The very fact that Mani set aside so summarily every element of Judaism that he encountered in the current Christianity, doubtless commended his views to a large and influential element in the East and the West alike. Mani claimed to set forth a spiritual religion as opposed to a carnal. The asceticism of Manichæism was in the line of a widespread popular ascetical movement that was already in progress, and so commended it to many. The question as to the origin of evil, and as to the relation of the good, wise and powerful God to the evil that appears in the world, in man and in demons was never asked with more interest than during the early Christian centuries, and any party that should advance a moderately plausible theory was sure to receive its share of public attention. Mani professed to have a solution and the only possible solution of questions of this class, and however fantastic may have been the forms in which his speculations were set forth, they were doubtless all the more acceptable on this account in that semi-pagan age to many intelligent people. The fact that these forms satisfied so able a thinker as Mani undoubtedly was, would guarantee their acceptance by a large number both East and West. There was in the West at this time, and had been for centuries, a hankering after Oriental theosophy, the more extravagant the better. The widespread worship of Mithra was an excellent preparation for the more complete system of Mani. Manichæism and Neo-Platonism antagonized the Christianity of the fourth and fifth centuries from opposite sides, and those minds for whom Platonism had no charms were almost sure to be attracted by the theosophy of Mani. "How are we to explain," asks Harnack, "the rapid spread of Manichæism, and the fact that it really became one of the great religions? Our answer is, that Manichæism was the most complete Gnosis, the richest, most consequent and most artistic system formed based on the ancient Babylonian religion.... What gave strength to Manichæism was... that it united its ancient mythology and a thorough-going materialistic dualism with an exceedingly simple spiritual worship and a strict morality. On comparing it with the Semitic religions of nature, we perceive that it retained their mythologies, after transforming them into doctrines, but abolished all their sensuous cultus, substituting instead a spiritual worship as well as a strict morality.

Manichæism was thus able to satisfy the new wants of an old world. It offered revelation, redemption, moral virtue, and immortality [this last is very doubtful, if conscious immortality be meant], spiritual benefits based on the religion of nature. A further source of strength lay in the simple, yet firm social organization which was given by Mani himself to his new institution. The wise man and the ignorant, the enthusiast and the man of the world, could all find acceptance here, and there was laid on no one more than he was able and willing to bear."

The question as to the secret of the fascination that Manichæism could exercise even over the most intelligent Western minds, may receive a more concrete answer from the autobiographical account of Augustin's own relations to the party. What was it that attracted and enthralled, for nine years, him who was to become the greatest theologian of the age? In his Confessions (Book III. ch. 6) he gives this impassioned account of his first connection with Manichæism: "Therefore I fell among men proudly railing, very carnal and voluble, in whose mouth were the snares of the devil—the bird lime being composed of a mixture of the syllables of Thy Name, and of our Lord Jesus Christ, and of the Paraclete, the Holy Ghost, the Comforter. These names departed not out of their mouths, but so far forth as the sound and clatter of the tongue; for the heart was empty of truth. Still they cried 'Truth, Truth,' and spoke much about it to me, yet it was not in them, but they spoke falsely not of Thee only—who, verily art the Truth—but also of the elements of this world, Thy creatures... O Truth, Truth! how inwardly even then did the marrow of my soul pant after Thee, when they frequently and in a multiplicity of ways, and in numerous and huge books, sounded out Thy Name to me, though it was but a voice. And these were the dishes in which to me, hungering for Thee, they, instead of Thee, served up the sun and the moon, Thy beauteous works—but yet Thy works, not Thyself, nay, nor Thy first works...Woe, woe, by what steps was I dragged down to the depths of hell!—toiling and turmoiling through want of Truth, when I sought after Thee, my God,—to Thee I confess it, who has mercy on me when I had not yet confessed, sought after Thee not according to the understanding of the mind in which Thou desires that I should excel the beasts, but according to the sense of the flesh."

Chapter IX.—Augustin and the Manichæans.

In the preceding Chapter we have given in Augustin's own words some account of the process by which he became ensnared in Manichæan error. In reading Augustin's account of his experience among the Manichæans, we cannot escape the conviction that he was never wholly a Manichæan, that he never surrendered himself absolutely to the system. He held it rather as a matter of opinion than as a matter of heart-attachment. Doubtless the fact that he continued to occupy himself with rhetorical and philosophical studies prevented his complete enthrallment. His mind was not naturally of an Oriental cast, and the study of the hard, common-sense philosophy of Aristotle, and of the Eclecticism of Cicero, could hardly have failed to make him more or less conscious of the absurdity of Manichæism. The influence of scientific studies on his mind is very manifest from Confessions, Book V. ch. 3, where he compares the accurate astronomical knowledge with which he had become acquainted, with the absurd cosmological fancies of Faustus, the great Manichæan teacher who appeared at Carthage in Augustin's twenty-ninth year. "Many truths, however, concerning the creation did I retain from these men [the philosophers], and the cause appeared to confirm calculations, the succession of seasons, and the visible manifestations of the stars; and I compared them with the sayings of Manichæus, who in his frenzy has written most extensively on these subjects, but discovered not any account either of the solstices, or the equinoxes, the eclipses of the luminaries, or anything of the kind I had learned in the books of secular philosophy. But therein I was ordered to believe, and yet it corresponded not with those rules acknowledged by calculation and by our light, but was far different."

From this time Augustin's faith was shaken, and he was soon able to throw off completely the yoke that had become too grievous to be borne. But to reject Manichæism was not necessarily to become an orthodox Christian. Augustin finds himself still greatly perplexed about the nature of God and the origin of evil, problems the somewhat plausible Manichæan solutions of which had ensnared him. It was through Platonism, or rather Neo-Platonism, that he was led to more just and satisfying views, and through Platonism, along with other influences, he was enabled at last to find peace in the bosom of the Catholic church. "And Thou, willing to show me how Thou 'resists the proud, but gives grace unto the humble,' and by how great an act of mercy Thou has pointed out to men the path of humility, in that 'Thy Word was made flesh and dwelt among men,'—Thou procures for me, by the instrumentality of one inflated with monstrous pride, certain books of the Platonists, translated from Greek into Latin. And therein I read not indeed in the same words but to the self-same effect, enforced by many and divers reasons, that 'In the beginning was the Word, and the Word was with God, and the Word was God. The same was in the beginning with God. All things were made by Him; and without Him was not anything made that was made.'" In other words, Augustin thought that he discerned complete harmony between the prologue of John's gospel and the teachings of the Platonists, and in this teaching, thus corroborated, he found the solution of the problem that had caused him such anguish of soul. In this connection Augustin points out in some detail the features that Platonism and Christianity have in common. Thus Neo-Platonism, not blindly followed, but adapted to his Christian purpose, became not only a means of deliverance to Augustin himself, but a mighty weapon for the combating of Manichæan error.

Neo-Platonism enters so largely and influentially into Augustin's polemics against Manichæism that it will be apposite here to inquire into the extent and the nature of Augustin's dependence on this system of thought. Much has been written on this subject, especially by German and French scholars. A brief statement of some of the more important points of contact is all that is allowable in an essay like this. Premising, therefore, that Platonism essentially influenced the entire circle of Augustin's theological and philosophical thinking, let us first examine the Neo-Platonic and Augustinian conceptions of God. With Augustin God is absolutely simple and immutable, incomprehensible by men in their present state of existence, exalted above all human powers of thought or expression. All things may be said of God, and yet nothing worthily; God is honored more by reverential silence than by any human voice. He is better known by not being known; it is easier to say what He is not, than what He is. God is wanting in qualities; has no variety and multitude of properties and attributes; is absolutely simple. By no means is God to be called substance, for the word substance pertains to a certain accident; nor is it allowable to think of Him as composed of substance and of accidents. Divine qualities are therefore purely subjective. There is no discrimination in God of substance and accidents, of potency and act, of matter and form, of universal and singular, of superior and inferior. To know, to will, to do, to be, are in God equivalent and identical. Eternity itself is the substance of God, which has nothing mutable, nothing past, nothing future. God makes new things, without being Himself new, unchangeable He makes changeable things, He always works and always rests. The changes that take place in the world do not fall in the will of God, but solely in the things moved by God. God changes them out of His unchangeable counsel. For nearly every one of these statements an almost exact parallel can be pointed out in the writings of Plotinus, the Neo-Platonic writer with whom Augustin was most conversant. It would be easy to point out that Augustin here goes to a dangerous extreme, and narrowly escapes fatalism on the one hand, and denial of the true personality of God on the other. But the effectiveness of this type of teaching against Manichæism is what chiefly interests us in this connection. Readers of the following treatises will have no difficulty in seeing for themselves how confidently and with what telling effect Augustin employs this view of God against the crudities of Manichæism, which thought of God as mutable, as capable of being successfully assailed by evil, as rent asunder, as suffering miserable contamination and imprisonment by mixture with matter, as painfully struggling for freedom, as suffering with the suffering of plants and animals, as liberated by their decay and by the digestive operations of the faithful, etc., etc.

Again, while still a Manichæan Augustin had thought and written much about beauty. On this point also, the throwing off of Manichæism and the adoption of a Platonizing Christianity brought about a revolution in his conceptions. The exactness with which he has followed Plotinus in his ideas of the beauty of God and of his creatures is remarkable. This we could fully illustrate by the citation of parallel passages. But we must content ourselves with remarking that Augustin himself acknowledged his indebtedness, and that his idea of beauty was an important factor in his polemics against Manichæism. According to Augustin (and Plotinus) God is the most beautiful and splendid of all beings. He is the beauty of all beauties; all the beautiful things that are the objects of our vision and love He Himself made. If these are beautiful what is He? All beauty is from the highest beauty, which is God. Augustin follows Plato and Plotinus even in neglecting the distinction between the good and the beautiful. The idea of Divine beauty Augustin applies to Christ also. He speaks of Him as beautiful God, beautiful Word with God, beautiful on earth, beautiful in the womb, beautiful in the hands of his parents, beautiful in miracles, beautiful in being scourged, beautiful when inciting to life, beautiful when not caring for death, beautiful when laying down his life, beautiful when taking it up again, beautiful in the sepulcher, beautiful in Heaven. The beauty of the creation, which is simply a reflection of the beauty of God, is not even disturbed by evil or sin. Beauty is with Augustin (and the Platonists) a comprehensive term, and is almost equivalent to perfect harmony or symmetry of parts, perfect adaptation of beings to the ends for which they exist.

It is patent that this view of the beauty of God and His creation is diametrically opposed to the crude conceptions of Mani, with reference to the disorder of the universe, a disorder not confined even to the Kingdom of Darkness, but invading the Realm of light itself. So also Augustin's Platonizing views of the creation must be taken into consideration in judging of his attitude towards Manichæism. It goes without saying that from Augustin's theological point of view, to account for creation is a matter of grave difficulty. How can there be a relation between the infinite and the finite? Any substantial connection is unthinkable. The only thing left is a relation of causality. The finite, according to Plotinus, is an accident, an image and shadow of God. It is constituted, established, sustained, and nourished by the Divine potency, and is therefore absolutely dependent upon God. The power that flows from God permeates each and every finite thing. God as one, whole, and indivisible, is perpetually present with his eternal process, to everything, everywhere. When Augustin teaches that God of his own free will, subject to no necessity, by His own Word created the world out of nothing, this statement might be taken regarding his view of the absolute simplicity of God and the consequent denial of distinction between being, willing, doing, etc. The easiest way to get over the difficulty involved in creation was to maintain the simultaneous creation of all things. The six days of creation in Genesis are an accommodation to human modes of thinking. In some expressions Augustin approaches the Platonic doctrine of the ideal or archetypal world. Finite things, so far as they exist, are essence, i.e., God; so far as they are not essence they do not exist at all. Thus, the distinction between God and the world is almost obliterated. Again, whatever is finite and derivative is subject to negation or nothingness. Thus, he goes along with Plato and Plotinus to the verge of denying the reality of derived existence, and so narrowly escapes pantheism.

It is easy to see how effectively this conception of creation might be employed against the Manichæan notion of the creation as something forced upon God by the powers of evil, and as a mere expedient for the gradual liberation of his imprisoned elements. The Manichæan limitation of God and his domain by the bordering Kingdom of Darkness, was in sheer opposition to Augustin's view of the indivisibility of God and his presence as a whole everywhere and always. Augustin's theory that nature or essence, as far as it has existence is God, is quite the antithesis of Mani's dualism, especially of his supposition that the Kingdom of Darkness is essentially and wholly evil. Augustin argued that even the inhabitants of the Kingdom of Darkness, and the King of Darkness himself, according to Mani's own representations, are good so far as they have essence or nature, and evil only so far as they are non-existent.

With Augustin's Platonizing view of creation is closely connected his theory of evil and his doctrine of divine providence. Evil with him, as with the Platonists, has no substantial existence. It is only privation of good. It is wanting in essence, substance, truth, —is in short mere negation, and so cannot have God for its efficient cause or author, or be referred to God. God would not have permitted evil unless by His own supreme power he had been able to make good use of it. He attempts, with some success, to show the advantages of the permission of evil in the world. God made all things good from the angels of heaven to the lowest beasts and herbs of the earth. Augustin delighted, with the Platonists, in dwelling upon the goodness of nature as shown in the animal and vegetable worlds, as well as in the great cosmical phenomena. Each creature of God has its place, some a higher, some a lower, but all so far as they conform to the idea of their creation, or to their nature, are good. So far as they fall short of this idea they are evil.

  This principle Augustin applied with great force to the confutation of the Manichæan view of the substantiality and permanence of evil. This may be regarded as the central point in Augustin's controversies with the Manichæans. He evidently felt that the Manichæan view of evil was the citadel of their system, and he never wearied of assailing it. It would be beyond the scope of the present essay to inquire whether and how far Augustin himself became involved in error, in his efforts to dislodge the Manichæans. Far less satisfactory than his confutation of the fundamental principles of the Manichæan system were his answers to the Manichæan cavils against the Old Testament. If we may judge from the prominence given in the extant literature to the Old Testament question, this must have been the favorite point of attack with the Manichæans. The importance of the questions raised and the necessity of answering them was fully recognized by Augustin. His principal reliance is the allegorical or typological method of interpretation. It would be hard to find examples of more perverse allegorizing than Augustin's Anti-Manichæan treatises furnish. It will not be needful to adduce instances here, as readers of the treatises will discover them in abundance. Nothing more wearisome and disgusting in Biblical interpretation can well be conceived of than certain sections of The Reply to Faustus, the Manichæan. Yet Augustin did not fail entirely to recognize the distinction between Old Testament times and New, and he even suggests the theory "that God could in a former age and to a people of a lower moral standard, give commands to do actions, which we should think it wrong to do now.... There was a certain inward want, an unenlightenment, a rudeness of moral conception, in those to whom such commands were given; otherwise they would not have been given. God would not have given a command to slaughter a whole nation to an enlightened people."

Yet with all the defects of Augustin's polemics against the Manichæans, they seem to have been adapted to the needs of the time. Well does Canon Mozley declare Augustin to have been "the most marvelous controversial phenomenon which the whole history of the Church from first to last presents.... Armed with superabundant facility of expression, —so that he himself observes that one who had written so much must have a good deal to answer for, —he was able to hammer any point of view which he wanted, and which was desirable as a counteracting one to a pervading heresy, with endless repetition upon the ear of the Church; at the same time varying the forms of speech sufficiently to please and enliven." Certainly, he was one of the greatest debaters of any age. He doubtless deserves the credit of completely checking the progress of Manichæism in the West, and of causing its gradual but almost complete overthrow. His arguments were probably more effective in guarding Christians against perversion by Manichæan proselytizers, than in converting those that were already ensnared by Manichæan error. Other controversies of a completely different character, especially the Pelagian, caused Augustin to look to other aspects of truth and so led to certain modifications in his own statements, nay led him on some occasions to the verge of Manichæan error itself. But we are chiefly interested at present in knowing that his earnest efforts against the Manichæans from A.D.388, the year of his baptism, to A.D. 405, were not in vain.

Chapter X.—Outline of Manichæan History.

In the East Mani's followers were involved in the persecution that resulted in his death, and many of them fled to Transoxiania. Their headquarters and the residence of the chief of the sect continued to be Babylon. They returned to Persia in 661, but were driven back, 908–32. They seem to have become very numerous in the Transoxiania. Albîrûnî, 973–1048, speaks of the Manichæans as still existing in large numbers throughout all Mohammedan lands, and especially in the region of Samarkand, where they were known as Sabeans. He also relates that they were prevalent among the Eastern Turks, in China, Thibet and India. In Armenia and Cappadocia they gained many followers, and thence made their way into Europe. The Paulicians are commonly represented as a Manichæan party, but the descriptions that have come down to us would seem to indicate Marcionitic rather than Manichæan elements. Yet contemporary Catholic writers such as Peter Siculus and Photius constantly assail them as Manichæans.

In the West we have traces of their existence from 287 onwards. Diocletian, according to a somewhat doubtful tradition, condemned its leaders to the stake, and its adherents to decapitation with confiscation of goods. The edict is supposed to have been directed to the proconsul of Africa where Manichæans were making great progress. According to an early account, Mani sent a special envoy to Africa. Valentinian (372) and Theodosius (381) issued bloody edicts against them, yet we find them still aggressive in the time of Augustin. From Africa Manichæism spread into Spain, Gaul and Aquitaine. Leo the Great and Valentinian III. took measures against them in Italy (440 sq.). They appear, however, to have continued their work, for Gregory the Great mentions them (590 sq.). From this time onwards, their influence is to be traced in such parties as the Euchites, Enthusiasts, Bogomiles, Catharists, Beghards, etc. But it is not safe to attach too much importance to the mere fact that these parties were stigmatized as Manichæans by their enemies. Even in the Reformation time and since, individuals and small parties have appeared which in some features strongly resembled the ancient Manichæans. Manichæism was a product of the East, and in the East it met with most acceptance. To the spirit of the West it was altogether foreign, and only in a greatly modified form could it ever have flourished there. It might persist for centuries as a secret society, but it could not endure the light.

Preface to the Anti-Manichæan Writings.

Introductory Essay on the Manichaean Heresy

No reader of the accompanying volume can be expected to take a very lively interest in its contents, unless he has before his mind some facts regarding the extraordinary genius to whom the heresy of Manichæism owes its origin and its name. His history is involved in considerable obscurity, owing to the suspicious nature of the documents from which it is derived, and the difficulty of constructing a consistent and probable account out of the contradictory statements of the Asiatics and the Greeks. The ascertained facts, therefore, are few, and may be briefly stated.

According to the Chronicle of Edessa, Mani was born A.D. 240. From his original name, Corbicius or Carcubius, Beausobre conjectures that he was born in Carcub, a town of Chaldæa. He belonged to a Magian family, and while still a youth won a distinguished place among the sages of Persia. He was master of all the lore peculiar to his class, and was, besides, so proficient a mathematician and geographer, that he could construct a globe. He was a skilled musician, and had some knowledge of the Greek language, —an accomplishment rare among his countrymen. But his fame, and even his ultimate success as a teacher, was due in great measure to his skill in painting, which was so considerable as to earn for him among the Persians the distinctive title, Mani the painter. His disposition was ardent and lively but patient and self-restrained. His appearance was striking, as he wore the usual dress of a Persian sage: the high-soled shoes, the one red, the other green; the mantle of azure blue, that changed color as he moved; the ebony staff in his right hand, and the Babylonish book under his left arm.

The meaning of his name, Mani, Manes, or Manichæus, has been the subject of endless conjectures. Epiphanius supposes that he was providentially so named, that men might be warned against the mania of his heresy. Hyde, whose opinion on any Oriental subject must have weight, tells us that in Persian mani means painter, and that he was so called from his profession. Archbishop Usher conjectured that it was a form of Manaemor Menahem, which means Paraclete or Comforter; founding this conjecture on the fact that Sulpicius Severus calls the Israelitish king Menahem, Mane. Gataker supplements this idea by the conjecture that Mani took this name at his own instance, and in pursuance of his claim to be the Paraclete. It is more probable that, if his name was really given because this meaning, he received it from the widow who seems to have adopted him when a boy, and may have called him her Consolation. But it is also possible that Mani was not an uncommon Persian name, and that he adopted it for some reason too trifling to discover.

While still a young man he was ordained as a Christian priest, and distinguished himself in that capacity by his knowledge of Scripture, and the zeal with which he discharged his sacred functions. His heretical tendencies, however, were very soon manifested, stimulated, we may suppose, by his anxiety to make the Christian religion more acceptable to those who adhered to the Eastern systems. Excommunicated from the Christian Church, Mani found asylum with Sapor, and won his confidence by presenting only the Magian side of his system. But no sooner did he permit the Christian element to appear, and call himself the apostle of the Lord, and show a desire to reform Magianism, than his sovereign determined to put him to death as a revolutionist. Forced to flee, he took refuge in Turkestan, and gained influence there, partly by decorating the temples with paintings. To lend his doctrines the appearance of divine authority, he adopted the same device as Zoroaster and Mohammed. Having discovered a cave through which there ran a rill of water, he laid up in it a store of provisions, and retired there for a year, giving out that he was on a visit to heaven. In this retirement he produced his Gospel, —a work illustrated with symbolical drawings the ingenuity of which has been greatly praised. This book Mani presented to Hormizdas, the son and successor of Sapor, who professed himself favorable to his doctrine, and even built him a castle as a place of shelter and retirement. Unfortunately for Mani, Hormizdas died in the second year of his reign; and though his successor, Varanes, was at first willing to shield him from persecution, yet, finding that the Magians were alarmed for their religion, he appointed a disputation to be held between the opposing parties. Such trials of dialectic in Eastern courts have not unfrequently resulted in very serious consequences to the parties engaged in them. In this instance the result was fatal to Mani. Worsted in argument, he was condemned to die, and thus perished in some sense as a martyr. The mode of his death is uncertain, but it seems that his skin was stuffed with chaff, and hung up in public in terrorem. This occurred in the year 277, and the anniversary was commemorated as the great religious festival of the Manichæans.

This is not the place to attempt any account or criticism of the strange eclecticism of Mani. An adequate idea of the system may be gathered from the accompanying treatises. It may, however, be desirable to give some account of the original sources of information regarding it.

We study the systems of heresiarchs at a disadvantage when our only means of ascertaining their opinions is from the fragmentary quotations and hostile criticism which occur in the writings of their adversaries. Such, however, is our only source of information regarding the teaching of Mani. Originally, indeed, this heresy was especially active in a literary direction, assailing the Christian Scriptures with an ingenuity of unbelief worthy of a later age, and apparently ambitious of promulgating a rival canon. Certainly, the writings of its early supporters were numerous; and from the care and elegance with which they were transcribed, the sumptuous character of the manuscripts, and the mysterious emblems with which they were adorned, we should fancy it was intended to inspire the people with respect for an authoritative though as yet undefined code. It is, indeed, nowhere said or implied that the sacred books of the Manichæans were reserved for the eye only of the initiated or elect; and their reception of the New Testament Scriptures (subject to their own revision and emendation) would make it difficult for them to establish any secret code apart from these writings. They were certainly, however, doctrines of an esoteric kind, which were not divulged to the catechumens or hearers; and many of their books, being written in Persian, Syriac, or Greek, were practically unavailable for the instruction of the Latin speaking population. It was not always easy, therefore, to obtain an accurate knowledge of their opinions. Commentaries on the whole of the Old and New Testaments were written by Hierax; a Theosophy by

Introductory Essay on the Manichaean Heresy

Aristocritus; a book of memoirs, or rather Memorabilia, of Mani, and other works, by Heraclides, Aphthonius, Adas, and Agapius. Unfortunately all of these books have perished, whether in the flames to which the Christian authorities commanded that all Manichæan books should be consigned, or by the slower if not more critical and impartial processes of time.

Mani himself was the author of several works: a Gospel, the Treasury of Life (and probably an abridgment of the same), the Mysteries, the Foundation Epistle, a book of Articles or heads of doctrine, one or two works on astronomy or astrology, and a collection of letters so dangerous, that Manichæans who sought restoration to the Church were required to anathematize them.

Probably the most important of these writings was the Foundation Epistle, so called because it contained the leading articles of doctrine on which the new system was built. This letter was written in Greek or Syriac; but a Latin version of it was current in Africa, and came into the hands of Augustin, who undertook its refutation. To accomplish this with the greater precision and effect, he quotes the entire text of each passage of the Epistle before proceeding to criticize it. Had Augustin accomplished the whole of his task, we should accordingly have been in possession of the whole of this important document. Unfortunately, for reasons unknown, Augustin stops short at an early point in the Epistle; and though he tells us he had notes on the remainder, and would someday expand and publish them, this promise lay unredeemed for thirty years till the day of his death. Extracts from the same Epistle and from the Treasury are also given by Augustin in the treatise De Natura Boni.

Next, we have in the Opus Imperfectum of

Augustin some extracts from a letter of Mani to Menoch, which Julian had unearthed and republished to convict Augustin of being still tainted with Manichæan sentiments. These extracts give us some insight into the heresiarch's opinions regarding the corruption of nature and the evils of sexual love.

Again, we have Mani's letter to Marcel, preserved by Epiphanius, and given in full by Beausobre; which, however, merely reiterates two of the doctrines most certainly identified with Mani, —the assertion of two principles, and the tenet that the Son of God was man only in appearance.

Finally, Fabricius has inserted in the fifth volume of his Bibliotheca Græcathe fragments, such as they are, collected by Grabe.

Such is the fragmentary character of the literary remains of Mani: for fuller information regarding his opinions we must depend on Theodoret, Epiphanius, Alexander of Lycopolis, Titus of Bostra, and Augustin. Beausobre is of opinion that the Fathers derived all that they knew of Manichæus from the Acts of Archelaus. This professes to be a report of a disputation held between Manes and Archelaus, bishop of Caschar in Mesopotamia. Grave doubts have been cast on the authenticity of this document, and Burton and Milman seem inclined to consider it an imaginary dialogue, and use it on the understanding that while some of its statements are manifestly untrustworthy, a discriminating reader may gather from it some reliable material.

In the works of Augustin there are some other pieces which may well be reckoned among the original sources. In the reply to Faustus, which is translated in this volume, the book of Faustus is not indeed reproduced; but there is no reason for doubting that his arguments are fairly represented, and we think there is evidence that even the original expression of them is preserved. Augustin had been acquainted with Faustus for many years. He first met him at Carthage in 383, and found him nothing more than a clever and agreeable talker, making no pretension to science or philosophy, and with only slender reading. His cleverness is sufficiently apparent in his debate with Augustin; the objections he leads are plausible, and put with acuteness, but at the same time with a flippancy which betrays a want of earnestness and real interest in the questions. In his reply to Faustus, Augustin is very much on the defensive, and his statements are apologetic rather than systematic.

But in an age when the ability to read was by no means commensurate with the interest taken in theological questions, written discussions were necessarily supplemented by public disputations. These theological contests seem to have been a popular entertainment in North Africa; the people attending in immense crowds, while reporters took down what was said on either side for the sake of appeal as well as for the information of the absent. In two such disputations Augustin engaged relating to Manichæism. The first was held on the 28th and 29th of August, 392, with a Manichæan priest, Fortunatus. To this encounter Augustin was invited by a deputation of Donatists and Catholics, who were alike alarmed at the progress which this heresy was making in the district of Hippo. Fortunatus at first showed some reluctance to meet so formidable an antagonist, but was prevailed upon by his own sectaries, and shows no nervousness during the debate. His incompetence, however, was manifest to the

Manichæans themselves; and so hopeless was it to think of any further proselytizing in Hippo, that he left that city, and was too much ashamed of himself ever to return. The character of his reasoning is shifty; he evades Augustin's questions and starts fresh ones. Augustin pushes his usual and fundamental objection to the Manichæan system. If God is impassable and incorruptible, how could He be injured by the assaults of the kingdom of darkness? In opposition to the statement of Fortunatus, that the Almighty produces no evil, he explains that God made no nature evil, but made man free, and that voluntary sin is the grand original evil. The most remarkable circumstance in the discussion is the desire of Fortunatus to direct the conversation to the conduct of the Manichæans, and the refusal of Augustin to make good the charges which had been made against them, or to discuss anything but the doctrine.

Twelve years after this, a similar disputation was held between Augustin and one of the elect among the Manichæans, who had come to Hippo to propagate his religion. This man, Felix, is described by Augustin as being ill-educated, but more adroit and subtle than Fortunatus. After a keen discussion, which occupied two days, the proceedings terminated by Felix signing a recantation of his errors in the form of an anathema on Mani, his doctrines, and the seducing spirit that possessed him. These two disputations are valuable, as exhibiting the points of the Manichæan system to which its own adherents were accustomed to direct attention, and the arguments on which they specially relied for their support.

The works given in the accompanying volume comprehend by no means the whole of Augustin's writings against this heresy. Before his ordination he wrote five anti-Manichæan books, entitled, De Libero Arbitrio, De Genesi contra Manichæos, De Moribus Ecclesiæ Catholicæ, De Moribus Manichæorum, and De Vera Religione. These Paulinus called his anti-Manichæan Pentateuch. After his ordination he was equally diligent, publishing a little treatise in the year 391, under the title De Utilitate Credendi, which was immediately followed by a small work, De Duabus Animabus. In the following year the report of the Disputatio contra Fortunatum was published; and after this, at short intervals, there appeared the books Contra Adimantum, Contra Epistolam Manichæi quam vocant Fundamenti, Contra Faustum, Disputatio contra Felicem, De Naturo Boni, and Contra Secundinum.

Besides these writings, which are exclusively occupied with Manichæism, there are others in which the Manichæan doctrines are handled with more or less directness. These are the Confessions, the 79th and 236th Letters, the Lecture on Psalm 140, Sermons 1, 2, 12, 50, 153, 182, 237, the Liber de Agone Christiano, and the De Continentia.

Of these writings, Augustin himself professed a preference for the reply to the letter of Secundinus. It is a pleasing feature of the times, that a heretic whom he did not know even by sight should write to Augustin entreating him to abstain from writing against the Manichæans, and reconsider his position, and ally himself with those whom he had till now fancied to be in error. His language is respectful, and illustrates the esteem in which Augustin was held by his contemporaries; though he does not scruple to insinuate that his conversion from Manichæism was due to motives not of the highest kind.

We have not given this letter and its reply, because the preference of Augustin has not been ratified by the judgment of his readers.

The present volume gives a fair sample of Augustin's controversial powers. His nine years' personal experience of the vanity of Manichæism made him thoroughly earnest and sympathetic in his efforts to disentangle other men from its snares, and also equipped him with the knowledge requisite for this task. No doubt the Pelagian controversy was more congenial to his mind. His logical acuteness and knowledge of Scripture availed him more in combating men who fought with the same weapons, than in dealing with a system which threw around its positions the mist of Gnostic speculation, or veiled its doctrine under a grotesque mythology, or based itself on a cosmogony too fantastic for a Western mind to tolerate. But however Augustin may have misconceived the strange forms in which this system was presented, there is no doubt that he comprehended and demolished its fundamental principles; that he did so as a necessary part of his own personal search for the truth; and that in doing so he gained possession, vitally and permanently of ideas and principles which subsequently entered into all he thought and wrote. In finding his way through the mazes of the obscure region into which Mani had led him, he once for all ascertained the true relation subsisting between God and His creatures, formed his opinion regarding the respective provinces of reason and faith, and the connection of the Old and New Testaments, and found the root of all evil in the created will. The Editor. Some knowledge of the Magianism of the time of Mani may be obtained from the sacred books of the Parsis, especially from the Vendidad Sade, an account of which

Introductory Essay on the Manichaean Heresy

is given by Dr. Wilson, of Bombay, in his book on the Parsi Religion.—Tr.

www.ingramcontent.com/pod-product-compliance
Lightning Source LLC
Chambersburg PA
CBHW052113070526
44584CB00017B/2458